The Little Book of
BUTTERFLIES

**BUSHEL
& PECK
BOOKS**

Text copyright © 2022 by Christin Farley

Published by Bushel & Peck Books, www.bushelandpeckbooks.com.
All rights reserved. No part of this publication may be reproduced without written
permission from the publisher.

Bushel & Peck Books is dedicated to fighting illiteracy all over the world.
For every book we sell, we donate one to a child in need—book for book.
To nominate a school or organization to receive free books,
please visit www.bushelandpeckbooks.com.

Type set in Temeraire, Avenir Next, and Bebas.

Illustrations sourced from the Biodiversity Heritage Library. Other image credits as follows:
vine pattern: Nespola Designs/Shutterstock.com; graph paper background: Vector Image
Plus/Shutterstock.com; viceroy butterfly: Shutterstock.com/KellyNelson; queen butterfly:
JMCA.photo/Shutterstock.com; butterfly icon: Fan dana/Shutterstock.com;
cover and title page butterflies: The Graphics Fairy.

Animal taxonomy sourced from Wikipedia.

ISBN: 9781638191438

First Edition

Printed in the United States

10 9 8 7 6 5 4 3 2 1

The Little Book of
BUTTERFLIES

CHRISTIN FARLEY

Contents

HUNGRY HUNTERS

In order to store enough food to go through metamorphosis, monarchs have to consume A LOT, gaining up to 2,700 times their original weight!

1. MONARCH

With their orange and black wings and the white dots on their wing tips, monarch butterflies are one of the most recognizable butterfly species in North America. Similar to birds, monarchs are the only butterflies known to make a phenomenal two-way migration, sometimes covering 3,000 miles! The eastern North American population migrates to Mexico for the winter months, while the western North American population flies from southern Canada down to California's Pacific Coast between Santa Cruz and San Diego. Travel occurs during the day, and the butterflies will roost in large colonies at night. Such roosting locations are used year after year. One of the most popular roosting spots is in Pismo Beach, CA, where up to 60,000 monarchs thrive in the eucalyptus trees during the winter season.

CLASSIFICATION

KINGDOM: *Animalia*

PHYLUM: *Arthropoda*

CLASS: *Insecta*

ORDER: *Lepidoptera*

FAMILY: *Nymphalidae*

GENUS: *Danaus*

SPECIES: *D. plexippus*

FADED GLORY

If you happen to see a less vibrant monarch, just know that their loss of color comes from scales that have fallen off after flying for a long period of time.

DISTINGUISHING DOTS

One way to differentiate between a male and female monarch is to look for two black dots on the lower part of each wing. Only the male monarchs have these markings.

7

SHORT-TERM

The spring azure butterfly is known to have one of the shortest lifespans of all the butterfly species, only surviving a few days as an adult.

Spring
Azure

2. SPRING AZURE

An early spring appearance characterizes the spring azure. Although found in many parts of North America, they are more prevalent in the eastern United States. Identifying characteristics of the spring azure include their small size of approximately one inch and blue wings. Males are typically brighter, while females sport a darker shade of blue with black margins on their forewings. The undersides of spring azures are pale gray with small, dark spots. And in larvae form, colors vary from downy green to reddish-brown to yellow-green. Spring azure adults take nectar from springtime flowers like milkweeds and wild plums, while the caterpillars eat the fruits and flowers found in deciduous woods, fields, and freshwater marshes.

KINGDOM: *Animalia*

PHYLUM: *Arthropoda*

CLASS: *Insecta*

ORDER: *Lepidoptera*

FAMILY: *Lycaenidae*

GENUS: *Celastrina*

SPECIES: *C. ladon*

HYPER-FOCUSED

Once they emerge from their chrysalis, time begins ticking for the spring azure. To be able to continue their species, they must quickly mate and lay eggs before their death.

Spring Azure

ANT ASSISTANCE

Caterpillars are often tended to by tree ants who protect them from predators while feeding on the caterpillars' sugary excretions.

3. GATEKEEPER

Gatekeeper butterflies make their homes across England, Wales, and Southern Ireland, where they get their name from their love of gateway flowers. They can be found in groups called a "kaleidoscope," with populations of dozens or even thousands. While many butterfly species come in orange and brown patterns, the gatekeeper is unique for the black eyespot on the edge of its forewings with two white dots inside. Peaceful insects, gatekeepers fly up to ten miles per hour with the simple goal of mating or finding nectar. Males produce pheromone chemicals to attract females, while both are drawn to their favorite nectar sources—ragwort and bramble.

COLOR OPTIONS

Not all gatekeepers inherit the orange and brown coloring. There are actually about 12 variations of color depending on their diet and habitat.

WINTER NAP

As small caterpillars, gatekeepers will go to sleep in September and do not conclude their hibernation until March. After a couple of months of eating, they will go into their pupa or chrysalis stage.

4. CABBAGE BUTTERFLY

CLASSIFICATION

KINGDOM: *Animalia*

PHYLUM: *Arthropoda*

CLASS: *Insecta*

ORDER: *Lepidoptera*

FAMILY: *Pieridae*

GENUS: *Pieris*

SPECIES: *P. brassicae*

Also known as the small white butterfly, cabbage butterflies get their name for depositing their larvae on cabbage plants. These white beauties are covered with fine hair and have distinct black markings on their pale wings. This species is found in abundance worldwide, from North America to Europe, Australia, and Asia. Cabbage butterflies are most likely to be seen in open spaces like farmland and fields. Here, females will lay their eggs on crops like cabbage, broccoli, kale, and other leafy greens. When the larvae, or caterpillars, are born, they begin to vigorously feast on their host plant. Farmers consider the cabbage butterfly to be an invasive pest that causes harm to their crops. As such, while parasitic flies are a natural threat to the butterflies, they are helpful to farmers in controlling the cabbage population.

MULTIGENERATIONAL

Two generations of cabbage butterflies are born in the space of a year. The first group appears in April–May, while the second follows in July–August.

COLOR PREFERENCE

Cabbage butterflies also feed on the nectar of flowers. It's been discovered that they prefer purple, blue, and yellow flowers over most others.

NAME GAME

Mourning cloak butterflies get their name from their appearance. Their coloring resembles a traditional cloak worn by those grieving the death of a loved one.

5. MOURNING CLOAK

If you live in the northwestern part of the United States, you might recognize a mourning cloak butterfly. As the state butterfly of Montana, the mourning cloak is easily distinguished from other species. Reddish-brown wings of about three inches boast glimmering blue spots on the inner edge of their beige border. With their wings upright, the dark brown underside with lighter edges is visible. The life of a mourning cloak includes four life stages—egg, larva, pupa, and adult. They are one of the longest-living adult butterflies in the world, surviving up to ten months! Tree sap is their main food source, and it is usually plentiful after seeping out of tree bark over the winter. With plenty of sap, the mourning cloaks wake early from hibernation and can be seen in early spring.

WARM START

Just like an old car's engine, mourning cloaks need to warm up before they start their flight. Angling its body toward the sun enables the butterfly to absorb heat.

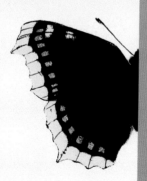

WINTER VACATION

Winter for a mourning cloak is spent in a mild state of hibernation until the weather starts to warm. Tree cavities provide a safe place for their winter slumber.

TAINTED TASTEBUDS

It's common
for most adult
butterflies to feed
on nectar. Viceroys
are different in that
they also will eat
fungus, carrion, and
feces.

Viceroy

6. VICEROY

A monarch butterfly look-alike, the viceroy butterfly sports a similar orange and black striping pattern. The viceroy is found throughout most of the United States and parts of Central Mexico. Marshes, meadows, and wetlands are their preferred habitat as they prefer to lay their eggs on the leaves of poplar and willow trees. Such leaves provide excellent nutrition for the black and white viceroy caterpillars. In fact, since they don't migrate, adult viceroys will wrap themselves up in such leaves to hibernate during the winter. If you spot one, you can tell them apart from a monarch by their size (viceroys are smaller than monarchs) and their flight. Their quick and erratic flight patterns greatly differ from a monarch's tendency to float and glide.

CAN YOU SPOT THE DIFFERENCE?

Look at the viceroy butterfly on the left and the monarch below. Can you see the difference in their wing patterns? The viceroy has an extra band of black midway through the wing.

Monarch

EYE-CATCHING CAUTION

The coloring of a viceroy is not just pleasing to the eye. It also serves as a defense against predators. Its bright color gives off the message that they are toxic or distasteful.

Giant
Hairstreak

1

2

Giant
Hairstreak

3

Regal
Hairstreak

4

Regal
Hairstreak

7. HAIRSTREAK

There are about 20 different documented species of hairstreak butterflies dispersed throughout the world, with the exception of Antarctica. Some of the well-known types are gray, white-letter, and green hairstreaks. The identifying characteristic of all hairstreaks is the slender, tail-like extension on their hindwings. Most abundantly found in the New World tropics like Central and South America, the small and delicate hairstreaks are known to be erratic fliers. While most are harmless, the larvae (or caterpillars) of the American gray hairstreak are harmful to farmers and their crops. With lovely coloring of reddish-brown or green, the larvae bore into seed and fruit, resulting in substantial losses.

CLASSIFICATION

KINGDOM: *Animalia*

PHYLUM: *Arthropoda*

CLASS: *Insecta*

ORDER: *Lepidoptera*

FAMILY: *Lycaenidae*

TRIBE: *Eumaeini*

GENUS: *Strymon*

LARVAE LIFE

The larvae of hairstreak butterflies are broad, short, and slug-like. While they eat plants, some species are cannibalistic.

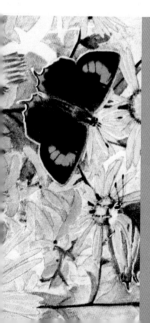

CONTINUALLY LEARNING

While we know the wingspan of a hairstreak is just over one inch, there is still much we don't know about them. Their litter size and flight speeds remain unknown.

Brown Hairstreak

PATIENT PARENTING

A female orange sulfur will only lay one of her many tiny white eggs at a time onto vegetation. Over her life, she will lay up to 1,000 eggs!

8. ORANGE SULFUR

Orange sulfurs are a widespread butterfly species also known as "alfalfa butterflies." They are spread across much of North America and play an important role in pollination as they flutter from flower to flower in search of nectar. From the mountains to the coasts, orange sulfurs like open habitats—anywhere with meadows, pastures, or agricultural fields. Their appearance is characterized by a yellowish-orange hue and their medium-size wingspan of around two inches. Sometimes, these and other butterflies can be mistaken for moths. If you find yourself uncertain, just look at their antennae. Butterfly antennae are slender with a club on the end, while those of moths can be feathery or threadlike with no club at their edge.

KINGDOM: *Animalia*

PHYLUM: *Arthropoda*

CLASS: *Insecta*

ORDER: *Lepidoptera*

FAMILY: *Pieridae*

GENUS: *Colias*

SPECIES: *C. eurytheme*

CRAFTY CAMOUFLAGE

Caterpillars are found in greater numbers from spring to fall. Coiled plants and vegetables serve as sulfur hiding places from predators or harsh weather.

SURVIVAL OF THE FITTEST

Orange sulfurs contribute to the food chain by providing a tasty meal for lizards, frogs, spiders, mice, and even carnivorous plants!

Tiger Swallowtail

SERIOUS SIZE

The giant swallowtail is the largest butterfly species in North America. With a wingspan of six inches, this black butterfly with yellow spots is sure to catch your eye!

9. SWALLOWTAILS

With over 500 species, swallowtail butterflies are found worldwide (save for Antarctica). Color combinations appear endless, but the main identifying characteristic of swallowtails is the tail-like extensions on their hindwings, resembling the forked tail of a swallow bird. In fact, the award for the longest tail-like extension goes to the zebra swallowtail; theirs can grow up to an inch. Other popular species are the Alpine black, Canadian tiger, eastern tiger, citrus, and spicebush swallowtails. While the vast majority of the species inhabit tropic regions, some are only found in certain regions of the globe. For example, only about 30 of the 500 swallowtail species are found in North America. Although the exact location varies, all species prefer to live in marshy areas and open grasslands.

CLASSIFICATION

KINGDOM: *Animalia*

PHYLUM: *Arthropoda*

CLASS: *Insecta*

ORDER: *Lepidoptera*

SUPERFAMILY: *Papilionoidea*

FAMILY: *Papilionidae*

POPULAR POSTAGE

One of the most well-known swallowtail species, the eastern tiger, has been displayed on a U.S. postage stamp twice!

Common
Banded
Peacock

COOL FOR SCHOOL

Many teachers raise painted lady butterflies in their classrooms as an educational experience for their students. A wide range of host plants makes them an easy species to raise.

10. PAINTED LADY

The painted lady is another orange and black butterfly that comes in spectacular patterns. "Cosmopolitan" and "thistle butterflies" are other names for the painted lady. The reason for the alternative titles is because of their global distribution (cosmopolitan) and the fact that thistle is one of the painted ladies' favorite foods. Incredibly unique, these butterflies can travel 100 miles a day at up to 30 mph, though sometimes only 6-12 feet off the ground. Unlike other butterfly species, painted ladies have unusual migration habits, independent of any season or geographical pattern. Some studies contribute their unique travel patterns to El Niño climates or the overpopulation of their species. On sunny days, you can find painted ladies in open areas full of colorful flowers; otherwise, if the sky is overcast, they are huddled in small depressions.

CLASSIFICATION

KINGDOM: *Animalia*

PHYLUM: *Arthropoda*

CLASS: *Insecta*

ORDER: *Lepidoptera*

FAMILY: *Nymphalidae*

GENUS: *Vanessa*

SPECIES: *V. cardui*

SILK SPINNERS

Similar to spiders, these caterpillars have a "spinneret" which they use to excrete liquid silk that quickly turns solid. Super strong natural fibers, the silk is used to construct the butterflies' web-like nests.

WARDROBE CHANGES

Before entering the chrysalis stage, the painted lady caterpillar will molt four times as it grows and its skin becomes too tight.

Silver-
Spotted
Skipper

NOT BOLD, BUT STILL BEAUTIFUL

Unlike other butterfly types, skippers tend to be dull in appearance. Black, white, brown, and gray are typical skipper colors.

11. SKIPPERS

With over 3,500 species, skipper butterflies come in many varieties. As such, they can be found in woodland glades and grasslands in Europe as well as both North and South America, depending on the subspecies. Others, like the regent skipper, inhabit Australia, and the Essex skipper inhabits the Middle East. The main commonalities between species are their stout bodies, small heads, large compound eyes, and antennae clubs that hook backward. Adult skippers generally eat nectar, grass, bird droppings, and flowers. Mud is even on the menu if they are in need of minerals. On the flip side, adult skippers make a tasty meal for spiders, dragonflies, and wasps, while caterpillars are sought out by praying mantises, wasps, and assassin bugs.

CLASSIFICATION

KINGDOM: *Animalia*

PHYLUM: *Arthropoda*

CLASS: *Insecta*

ORDER: *Lepidoptera*

SUPERFAMILY: *Papilionoidea*

FAMILY: *Hesperiidae*

LONGING FOR LARVAE

How do fried and canned caterpillar larvae sound for dinner? In parts of Mexico, this is considered a delicacy and is called "gusanos de maguey."

NAME ORIGIN

Why is a skipper called a "skipper?" The butterflies get their name from their quick, skipping flight style.

PECULIAR PUPA

The pupa stage for the question mark is spent inside its chrysalis. Such pupae are known to take on the color of their surroundings to camouflage from predators.

12. QUESTION MARK

A North American native, the question mark butterfly can be found from Canada to Mexico, though they are absent from New Jersey, Florida, and New York City. They inhabit parks, residential landscapes, and moist woodlands. Their forewings are bright orange with dark spots, while their wing tips are grayish-white. Question marks get their name from the row of three black spots on their sharply angled wings, paired with an elongated dash that resembles the punctuation mark. Sometimes, the mark can even be silver. Medium-to-large-sized, the question mark has a wingspan of about 2.5 inches and only lives 6-20 days after it reaches adulthood. Its short adult lifespan is spent searching for a mate and laying eggs before it dies.

CLASSIFICATION

KINGDOM: *Animalia*

PHYLUM: *Arthropoda*

CLASS: *Insecta*

ORDER: *Lepidoptera*

FAMILY: *Nymphalidae*

GENUS: *Polygonia*

SPECIES: *P. interrogationis*

UNDERCOVER SIDE

The underside of a question mark butterfly is a blotchy brown. Such coloration lets it blend in with dry leaves and branches.

LIGHTWEIGHT

An adult question mark butterfly only weighs around .01 ounces. This is less than the weight of a cotton ball or three popcorn kernels.

HANGING AROUND

Common buckeye pupae sport a dark brown chrysalis to blend in with the surrounding twigs and branches where they hang for one to two weeks. Though it might sound idle, lots of changes are taking place inside!

13. COMMON BUCKEYE

As you wander through regions of the United States and Mexico butterfly hunting, you might feel like you are being watched. Why you might ask? Common buckeyes have three brightly colored, eye-like markings on both wings that are sure to make you feel a little uneasy. While feeling uneasy might be an exaggeration, these eye-like markings (called "eyespots") do play an important role in their defense. Common buckeye markings make predators think they are facing a larger and more intimidating predator. Caterpillars in the larval stage are also intricate in design. Their 1.5-inch bodies are black with orange-cream spots on their sides and blue, spine-like structures on their backs.

CLASSIFICATION

KINGDOM: *Animalia*

PHYLUM: *Arthropoda*

CLASS: *Insecta*

ORDER: *Lepidoptera*

FAMILY: *Nymphalidae*

GENUS: *Junonia*

SPECIES: *J. coenia*

FOODIE FAVORITES

Popular buckeye hot spots for flower nectar include tickseed sunflowers, knapweed, chicory, aster, and gumweed flowers.

NASTY NUTRITION

Caterpillars consume plants rich in "iridoid glycoside," a bitter-tasting chemical compound, as it makes them less desirable as food to birds, wasps, and small animals.

Red admiral butterflies are not afraid of people and are generally friendly. Don't be surprised if they perch on your arms, head, or shoulders! If you want them to leave, give a gentle blow of air their way.

14. RED ADMIRAL

While it sounds like it is named after a navy commander, the red admiral actually gets its name from the reddish band on its forewing. The other main red admiral colors are black and orange with white spots on the top edges. Scalloped edges give the red admiral a delicate look to match its small stature. Its global distribution reaches from North America to Europe and from Asia to Africa. They can thrive in forests, seashores, marshes, cities, and even homes. Attracted to warmth, those in colder climates have to migrate in the winter, while those in warmer climates can wait things out at home. Red admiral adults feed on tree sap, rotting fruit, and bird droppings. If those food sources grow scarce, they will turn to flower nectar.

TRICKY TRACKING

Trying to follow a red admiral in-flight might make you dizzy! These fidgety flyers are difficult to track with your sight as they rapidly change directions in the air.

CLOSE COUSINS

There are other admiral butterflies in the world! The Weidemeyer's admiral is found in the western United States, while the white admiral lives in North America, Great Britain, Japan, and Eurasia. The Canary Islands and India also serve as homes for the Indian red admiral.

MEANINGFUL NAME

California sisters get their name for their black wing parts and white band. The pattern resembles the headdress of religious nuns.

15. CALIFORNIA SISTER

With so many varieties of butterflies, it can be a challenge to distinguish between species, especially when spring rolls around. So, if you are looking to find a California sister, here's a helpful hint: look for the orange patches on the tips of the forewings and a creamy white vertical band down the wings, mimicking a "V" shape. With various colors on their underside, the California sister is sure to impress! They glide through the forests and woodlands of the West Coast of the United States, Nevada, and parts of Mexico. Unlike many butterfly species, California sisters rarely sip nectar and would rather consume overripe fruit.

CLASSIFICATION

KINGDOM: *Animalia*

PHYLUM: *Arthropoda*

CLASS: *Insecta*

ORDER: *Lepidoptera*

FAMILY: *Nymphalidae*

GENUS: *Adelpha*

SPECIES: *A. californica*

PICKY PALATE

Caterpillars are picky about their host plants. California sisters are all about oaks! They prefer the leaves of the coast live oak and the canyon live oak.

POSTERITY PREVALENCE

The California sister species can produce anywhere from one to three generations per year. They are most visible from March–November, though some will wade out the winter months.

AGGRESSIVE AGING

Zebra longwings grow up so fast! If the weather conditions are right, they can grow from egg to adult in a little over three weeks!

16. ZEBRA LONGWING

Zebra longwings are medium-to-large butterflies found in South and Central America and as far north as southern Texas and Florida. They are attracted to moist and warm tropical habitats where there is an abundance of flower nectar to sip. Narrow black wings with light-yellow stripes give this butterfly its name. Caterpillars are similar in appearance to their adult counterparts, with a white body, black spots, and black, spine-like structures on their backs. One of their more unusual traits is that they feed on highly nutritious pollen as well as nectar. This modification provides them a longer life than their nectar-only consuming cousins. Another interesting fact is that they are famous! Zebra longwings are the state butterfly of Florida!

NIGHTLIFE

Zebra longwings are social insects. In the evening, large groups will roost together in the same trees night after night as a protection from predators.

PASSIONATE PREFERENCES

Passionflower leaves are a favorite food source for caterpillars. While tasty, the toxins in the leaves make them poisonous and unappetizing to predators.

17. GREAT SPANGLED FRITILLARY

Medium in size with about a three-inch wingspan, the great fritillary butterfly is the most common of the fritillary species in North America. It can thrive in southern regions of Canada to Northern California and from the west to the east coast of the United States. Adults enjoy moist meadows and woodlands as their homes, where they fit into the habitat with their orange and brownish-tan coloring. The caterpillar sports a much more aggressive design. Black, spike-like structures and orange nodules on their black backs make them look ready for war! Instead, these mild creatures prefer a quiet life consuming the delicious flowers of their host—violet plants.

SUMMER FLING

Great fritillary butterflies must know when school gets out and summer begins because they show up for the party! They are most active from mid-June to mid-September.

GARDEN GUESTS

Large numbers of fritillaries are known to populate home gardens. If this sounds intriguing, check out your local garden center. They have flower sections devoted to butterfly gardens.

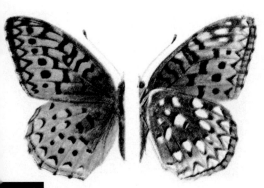

18. CALIFORNIA DOGFACE

CLASSIFICATION

KINGDOM: *Animalia*

PHYLUM: *Arthropoda*

CLASS: *Insecta*

ORDER: *Lepidoptera*

FAMILY: *Pieridae*

GENUS: *Zerene*

SPECIES: *Z. eurydice*

If you've ever been to California, you have probably seen the California dogface butterfly. Endemic to the state, the dogface is also the state insect! "Dogface" is a peculiar name for a butterfly, but if you spot a male dogface, you will understand the significance of its name. The upper wings are iridescent blue-ish black with what looks like a dog's face in the middle (like a poodle). The lower wings are a lovely orange and yellow pattern. Dogfaces inhabit foothill regions and coniferous woodlands where they search for their main food source—flower nectar. Before their metamorphosis, dogfaces live as green caterpillars with pale green stripes. Their coloring helps them blend into their host plant.

FAVORED FLAVOR

Word on the street among butterfly enthusiasts is that dogfaces have a favorite color. Of the plentiful assortment of flowers they pass, they have a preference for purple!

SWIFT ESCAPE

Photographers have a difficult time capturing a dogface with its wings open. Their quick flight patterns also make hunting them difficult for predators like birds, frogs, lizards, and wasps.

CONFUSING COUSINS

It's totally normal to get a clouded sulfur mixed up with an orange sulfur butterfly. The main difference is the shade of color on their bodies. Orange sulfurs have an orangish hue, while clouded sulfurs are mainly yellow in color.

19. CLOUDED SULFUR

Sulfur is a chemical compound that is yellow in color with a rotten-egg smell that can clear a room. Thankfully, the clouded sulfur butterfly gets its name from the sulfur color and not the sulfur smell! Males and females are similar in appearance, with dull orange spots on their hindwings and single black spots on their forewings. They are widely dispersed and commonly found in North America, including up north in the Yukon. Medium in size, clouded sulfurs love the sun and can be found in clusters near pastures, country roads, and meadows. In fact, they have an affinity for water and are avid mudpuddlers! You can see them fluttering in search of their favorite flowers for nectar—milkweeds, goldenrods, dandelions, and clovers.

PAY IT FORWARD

As clouded sulfurs travel from flower to flower for nectar, they pass along pollen that gets on their bodies from their visits. Such pollination helps plant seeds to grow and spread.

INTERBREEDING ISSUES

Sometimes, clouded sulfurs (top) and orange sulfurs (bottom) interbreed. This hybridization produces sterile female offspring, meaning they cannot reproduce.

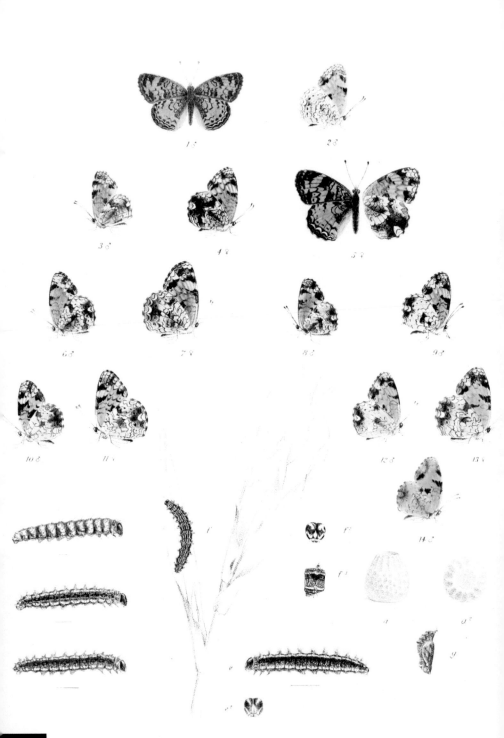

20. PEARL CRESCENT

Sometimes, pearl crescent butterflies can be difficult to distinguish from their cousins, the northern and tawny crescents. Pearl crescents, however, are one of the most widespread and common butterfly species in the United States. Perhaps their large numbers are due to the fact that two "broods" (generations) are born each year. Pearl crescents are mainly orange with dark brown edging and a complex design of brown lines and spots. A sliver of moon-shaped crescents is found toward the bottom of the hind wings before the dark outer border. This species inhabits forests and grasslands where they seek out aster plants, their favorite host plant, for eggs and caterpillars to thrive. Once they reach adulthood, pearl crescents will use their proboscis to siphon nectar from a variety of flowers.

CLASSIFICATION

KINGDOM: *Animalia*

PHYLUM: *Arthropoda*

CLASS: *Insecta*

ORDER: *Lepidoptera*

FAMILY: *Nymphalidae*

GENUS: *Phyciodes*

SPECIES: *P. tharos*

STRENGTH IN NUMBERS

Unlike many butterfly species, female pearl crescents lay their eggs together instead of singularly on the underside of plants. The average number of eggs in a litter is 36.

COLORFUL CHILDHOOD

Pearl crescents begin life as a green egg. As they progress as larvae, they appear brown with small, white spots. Colors change once again as they reach adulthood, shifting to yellow and dark brown.

COURTSHIP CUES

A male pearl crescent flies around patrolling host plants. Females will show their interest by spreading their wings as he passes, or they will keep them closed to signal their denial.

SURVIVAL STATUS

Recent decades have seen a decline in Duke of Burgundy numbers. They are currently a threatened species, known to inhabit only 20 sites in England.

21. DUKE OF BURGUNDY

Only found in England, the Duke of Burgundy is an elusive species and is even a rare sight for keen butterfly-spotters. Females spend most of their time flying close to the ground in search of suitable egg-laying sites. Males are the ones typically seen as they perch on leaves found in woodland clearings and scrubby grasslands. You can pick out a Duke from their primarily brown bodies and wings. Orange markings color the outer half of their wings. Black and white stripes adorn their antennae which have black knobs on the ends. Caterpillars are tiny and green, and they only feed at dusk. Primrose and cowslip are their two primary food sources.

CLASSIFICATION

KINGDOM: *Animalia*

PHYLUM: *Arthropoda*

CLASS: *Insecta*

ORDER: *Lepidoptera*

FAMILY: *Riodinidae*

SUBFAMILY: *Nemeobiinae*

TRIBE: *Zemerini*

GENUS: *Hamearis*

SPECIES: *H. lucina*

UNKNOWN ORIGIN

Duke of Burgundy butterflies get their name from artist and illustrator, Moses Harris. The name appeared for the first time in the second half of the 18th century, though it's unclear why Harris named them so.

ROYAL RECOGNITION

Their name suggests a mighty and imposing appearance. However, Duke of Burgundy butterflies are actually quite small, with wingspans of about one inch.

DEFENSE TACTICS

If danger is lurking nearby, peacocks will stay motionless, like a leaf, to blend into their surroundings. They can also make a hissing noise by rubbing their wings together. Combined with the eyespots, these are effective methods of deterring predators.

22. PEACOCK

If you are hoping to see a peacock butterfly in the winter, just hold tight! These beauties don't emerge from their chrysalis until late spring after their winter hibernation. Prevalent in Europe and Asia, peacocks enjoy temperate weather in woods and open fields. Popular creatures in the United Kingdom, peacocks are known for their large eyespots on each of their four wings, resembling a peacock's feathers. While caterpillars mainly feed on nettle plants, adults have a wider palate. Flowers of clover, willow, and dandelion provide needed nutrition along with rotten fruit and tree sap. Like other butterfly species, peacocks are important members of their ecosystems. They help to transfer pollen from flower to flower.

CLASSIFICATION

KINGDOM: *Animalia*

PHYLUM: *Arthropoda*

CLASS: *Insecta*

ORDER: *Lepidoptera*

SUPERFAMILY: *Papilionoidea*

FAMILY: *Nymphalidae*

OPTICAL ILLUSION

If you view a peacock butterfly upside down, you might see something unexpected. The wing pattern from this vantage point looks like an owl's face!

WINTER HIDEOUTS

Like other butterfly species, peacocks spend the winter months sleeping. Safe refuge from the weather is found in dead wood, hollow trees, and even attics!

CLOUD COVER

Overcast weather limits most butterflies' ability to fly since they need solar radiation. Ringlets are darker in color, allowing them to warm up faster so that they can fly in cloudy conditions.

23. RINGLET

There is a wide range of variety when it comes to ringlet butterflies. Their main identifying characteristic is the rings on their hindwings when they are at rest, giving them their name. With their wings open, you can see the ringlet's uniform chocolate color with white ridges around the wing tips. Variation in the species is usually due to the shape or the size of the ringlet. Sometimes, they are elongated to form a teardrop shape. Ringlets are inhabitants of the United Kingdom and Ireland. Most prefer shady and moist areas safe from the summer sun. Woodland edges and meadows provide them needed cover along with ample amounts of bramble, thistles, and fleabane for food.

CLASSIFICATION

KINGDOM: *Animalia*

PHYLUM: *Arthropoda*

CLASS: *Insecta*

ORDER: *Lepidoptera*

FAMILY: *Nymphalidae*

GENUS: *Aphantopus*

SPECIES: *A. hyperantus*

EGG DROP

A female ringlet lays her eggs in an unconventional way. Perched on a grass stem, she will randomly eject a single egg (usually in the air), where it will land in nearby vegetation.

TYPICAL TRAITS

Ringlets usually have five eyespot rings on the underside of their hindwings and three on the underside of the forewings.

24. PURPLE EMPEROR

CLASSIFICATION

KINGDOM: *Animalia*

PHYLUM: *Arthropoda*

CLASS: *Insecta*

ORDER: *Lepidoptera*

FAMILY: *Nymphalidae*

GENUS: *Apatura*

SPECIES: *A. iris*

As its name suggests, the purple emperor is both stately and majestic. Second only to swallowtails, they are the largest type of butterfly and even have males the size of small birds. To identify a purple emperor, look for patterns of dark brown and white for females and, for males, an additional bright blue on their dorsal wings. A small orange ring on the male or female's hindwings is also a clue to their identity. Similar to other caterpillars, the purple emperor eats leaves of their host plants, like sallow trees. Adults, however, do not drink the common flower nectar. Instead, they prefer to sip tree sap and honeydew that is produced by aphids.

HIGH FLYERS

Butterfly collectors in Europe have had to attach nets to 14-15 foot poles to catch these high flyers! If nets don't work, they have to use rotting animal carcasses to entice the males to fly down.

DOWNWARD TREND

Even though their numbers are in decline, purple emperors are not a threatened species. Thankfully, they are protected by the Wildlife and Countryside Act of 1981 (legislation in the U.K.).

GREEK MYTHOLOGY

The scientific name for the purple emperor is Apatura, meaning "the deceitful one" in Greek. The word was used to describe several Greek goddesses and probably refers to the male butterflies who only sometimes show their iridescent wings.

ALMOST EXTINCT

Due to large vegetation fires in 2013 and 2014, the northern brown argus habitat was extensively damaged. It was feared that the butterfly colonies would be completely wiped out. Thankfully, their numbers are starting to increase again!

25. NORTHERN BROWN ARGUS

Northern England and Eastern Scotland are the only places where you will find northern brown arguses. The climate and habitat are specifically tailored to the needs of this butterfly species. They can sun themselves in sheltered areas or on bare earth, or they can enjoy the limestone grasslands, coastal valleys, and quarries. Northern brown argus butterflies prefer these areas as they are home to their only larval foodplant, the common rock-rose. They are first placed on the common rock-rose as eggs and, within a couple of weeks, are devouring its leaves as caterpillars. These small United Kingdom favorites are dark brown with golden undertones. A furry, white border and a single white dot on each forewing make a lovely contrast with the orange markings on each wing.

CLASSIFICATION

KINGDOM: *Animalia*

PHYLUM: *Arthropoda*

CLASS: *Insecta*

ORDER: *Lepidoptera*

FAMILY: *Lycaenidae*

GENUS: *Aricia*

SPECIES: *A. artaxerxes*

PROTECTIVE PARTNERS

Ants and arguses have a symbiotic relationship. The larvae secrete nourishing and sweet liquid from special glands that the ants love. Equally beneficial is the protection the larvae receive from the ants' presence.

GENETIC FINDINGS

For decades, it was believed that the northern brown argus and the brown argus were the same species. Genetic studies now show they are two different and distinct species, though they share some similar traits.

Tortoiseshell butterflies are not afraid of cold weather. They hibernate during the winters and can withstand temperatures of -5 degrees Fahrenheit without freezing.

26. LARGE TORTOISESHELL

CLASSIFICATION

KINGDOM: *Animalia*

PHYLUM: *Arthropoda*

CLASS: *Insecta*

ORDER: *Lepidoptera*

FAMILY: *Nymphalidae*

GENUS: *Nymphalis*

SPECIES: *N. polychloros*

Once a common and widespread butterfly throughout Britain, the large tortoiseshell was thought to have gone extinct in the 1960s. Though sightings of this gorgeous creature are rare, its numbers are slowly increasing. With only one brood per year, adult butterflies emerge in mid-to-late summer and, soon after, hibernate for the winter months, only to then re-emerge in the spring. Shortly after waking from hibernation, the tortoiseshell will mate and begin the cycle all over again. To spot these butterflies, look for brown, furry bodies with golden-orange wings. Their dark, scalloped wing edges are decorated with faint blue markings. Their forewings also have medium-to-large dark blotches. You might find adults in woodlands with plenty of flowers for sipping nectar.

DETAILS OF DECLINE

What caused the large tortoiseshell to almost become extinct? One theory is that their primary food source, the Dutch elm, became diseased, affecting their ability to find food.

LONG-WINGED

You might guess one of the differences between a small and large tortoiseshell butterfly—their size! The large tortoiseshells have a larger wingspan of up to 3 inches versus 2.5 inches for the small tortoiseshell.

Comma caterpillars are a mix of white, orange, and black. Their patterns resemble bird droppings; this works as a defense against predators who turn away from them.

27. COMMA

When their wings are open, comma butterflies are brownish-orange with black blotches. With wings folded up, their brown and black wings resemble dead leaves. Another identifying characteristic of the comma is the white bulb-tip at the end of their dark antennas, resembling electric light. Most important, though, is the comma shape on the underside of their wings, giving them their deserving name. Comma butterflies inhabit areas of Europe, Asia, and North Africa where they can flourish in woodlands, gardens, and lightly forested areas. An interesting fact is that the shade of their wings can differ depending on when they emerge as adults. Those that emerge in early summer appear paler than those who appear later in the season.

WELCOME GARDEN

Would you like to have commas visit your home garden? Some of the best flowering plants to add to welcome them are lavender, wallflowers, ice plants, mint, and oregano.

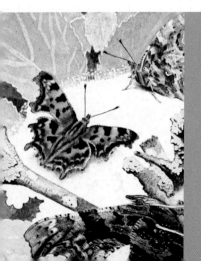

DELICIOUS DELIGHTS

Just as you might have your favorite foods, so do comma butterflies! Sweet tree sap and rotten or rotting fruit are just a few of their food faves.

COLOR CHANGING

Brimstone eggs are unusual in appearance. They are thin and spindle-shaped, and they can change color as they develop! From a greenish-white, they shift to dark yellow and, eventually, to brown before hatching.

Brimstone
Butterfly

28. BRIMSTONE

Brimstone butterflies have nearly completely solid-colored wings, setting them apart from the many multicolored butterfly species. The pale green color and noticeable veins of both wing sides make them almost unrecognizable from a leaf. Damp woodlands, hedgerows, and scrubby grasslands across Asia, Europe, and parts of Africa are where brimstones call home. Such areas usually come with an abundance of food like hawthorn, rowan, and blackthorn. Brimstone butterflies have a longer lifespan than most butterfly species, surviving for up to 13 months. Perhaps their longevity is due to the fact that they are fully protected under the Northern Ireland Wildlife Order of 1985. As a result, brimstones are not currently threatened and see low conservation efforts.

CLASSIFICATION

KINGDOM: *Animalia*

PHYLUM: *Arthropoda*

CLASS: *Insecta*

ORDER: *Lepidoptera*

FAMILY: *Pieridae*

TRIBE: *Goniopterygini*

GENUS: *Gonepteryx*

WORD-WISE

What does the word "dimorphic" mean in butterflies? This term means that males and females have apparent differences. For instance, only the wings of the male brimstone can change color under ultraviolet light.

IMITATORS

Both male and female brimstones have a tiny orange blotch on each wing called "fungal spots" to imitate such spots on real leaves.

HOME SWEET HOME

When they are not eating, American lady caterpillars make nests in their host plants. They produce silk that they use to sew together pieces of leaves and fluff. This allows them a place to rest from the elements.

29. AMERICAN LADY

American lady butterflies are medium-sized butterflies found on almost every continent with the exception of Antarctica. Originally native to the Canary Islands, their habitats range from fields and meadows to beach dunes and vacant lots. Look for them alone or in groups, living peaceful lives with only the occasional caterpillar causing problems for farmers' crops. American ladies look almost identical to their close cousins, the painted lady butterflies. With similar bright orange and dark brown wings, the only noticeable differences are the Americans' single white dot on the orange section of the forewing and their two hindwing eyespots instead of four. You can usually spot females flying low in search of host plants, while males sip moisture from nutrient-rich puddles.

CLASSIFICATION

KINGDOM: *Animalia*

PHYLUM: *Arthropoda*

CLASS: *Insecta*

ORDER: *Lepidoptera*

FAMILY: *Nymphalidae*

GENUS: *Vanessa*

SPECIES: *V. virginiensis*

BREATHING EASY

Without lungs, how do butterflies breathe? Like other species, American ladies have "spiracles," or tiny holes in the sides of their bodies. The holes lead to tubes, carrying the oxygen throughout their bodies.

INDIVIDUAL STYLE

American lady caterpillars have a look all their own. Their black bodies have multiple white stripes and two white dots at each body segment. They also have black, spike-like structures that make you want to keep your distance!

30. DREAMY DUSKYWING

With the exception of Mexico and Texas, the dreamy duskywing can be found in most areas of North America. These non-migratory butterflies like to keep to their home territories of moist forests and open woodlands. Dreamys get their whimsical titles from the lack of white dots on the edge of their dorsal front wings that other duskywing species have. Without the dots, they are known for their "closed eyes." As far as coloring goes, dreamys are entirely brown with hints of gray scales and dark spots. They blend in beautifully with tree bark and dead leaves when flying low. For host plants, dreamys mainly choose poplar and willow trees for depositing their eggs.

THIRD-PLACE FINISH

A study shows that the dreamy duskywing is the third most frequently found duskywing species. It falls behind the more common Juvenal's and wild indigo duskywing.

MAKING HISTORY

The dreamy duskywing species was first described in a paper presented at the Boston Society of Natural History. This 1870 discovery was made by Samuel Scudder and E. Burgess.

31. QUEEN

Aesthetically regal, the queen butterfly looks remarkably similar to its monarch cousin. Their wings are predominantly orange with black around the border and plentiful white dots on the outer edges. One of the largest butterfly species, the queen has a body length of two inches and a wingspan of up to 3.5 inches. Mudpuddlers, queen butterflies sip from puddles after it rains to rehydrate and absorb the salts from the soil. Male and female queen butterflies love milkweed flowers from the sunny open spaces of pastures and roadsides. Appearance is another thing males and females have in common. One of the only ways to tell them apart is through close observation. Males have two white dots on their hindwings that female queens lack.

CLASSIFICATION

KINGDOM: *Animalia*

PHYLUM: *Arthropoda*

CLASS: *Insecta*

ORDER: *Lepidoptera*

FAMILY: *Nymphalidae*

GENUS: *Danaus*

SPECIES: *D. gilippus*

LONG-DISTANCE CRAWLER

When the time comes to pupate (form a chrysalis), queen caterpillars may crawl up to 100 feet away from their host plant to find a proper place to attach themselves.

DISCOVERING DEFINITIONS

Here is a butterfly term to be familiar with: a "roost" is a group of butterflies that cluster together. They form a roost to keep warm at night and to camouflage against predators.

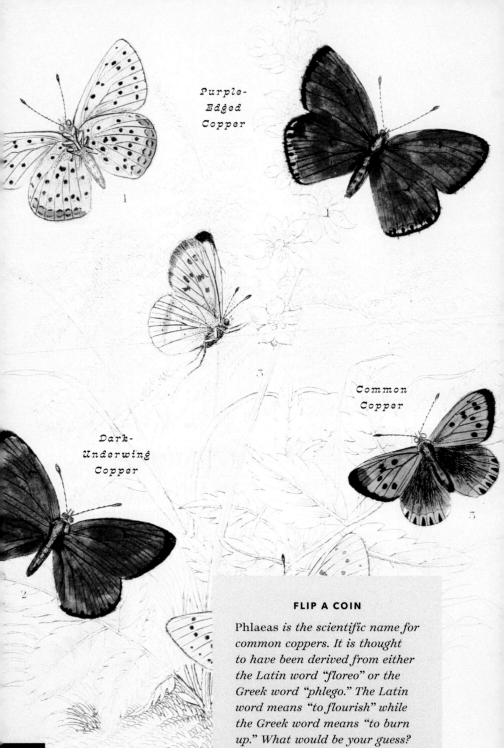

Purple-
Edged
Copper

1

Common
Copper

Dark-
Underwing
Copper

FLIP A COIN

Phlaeas *is the scientific name for common coppers. It is thought to have been derived from either the Latin word "floreo" or the Greek word "phlego." The Latin word means "to flourish" while the Greek word means "to burn up." What would be your guess?*

32. COMMON COPPER

Common coppers are part of the Lycaenidae family and are known for their contrasting black and bright-orange wings. Their hindwings are predominantly black while their forewings are mainly orange with black spots. Similar coloring exists on the underside, only the hues are fainter. The main difference between male and female common coppers is that females have fewer spots on their wings. Unlike other coppers, the common copper is widely dispersed around the globe. They thrive in heathlands and woodland clearings of North America, Asia, Europe, and parts of Africa. Bright, sunny days are when you can see coppers at their best! Even though their adult life only spams a quick two weeks, they enjoy their days sipping nectar and beautifying the world around them!

CLASSIFICATION

KINGDOM: *Animalia*

PHYLUM: *Arthropoda*

CLASS: *Insecta*

ORDER: *Lepidoptera*

FAMILY: *Lycaenidae*

GENUS: *Lycaena*

SPECIES: *L. phlaeas*

UNNERVED

Mating season is a particularly stressful time for males. They are so territorial that they will get agitated over just seeing shadows of large birds.

RESPECTABLE RELATIVES

If you have a fascination with common copper butterflies, you should learn more about their cousins. The bronze copper and American copper are both commonly dispersed in the United States.

33. BALTIMORE CHECKERSPOT

Baltimore checkerspots are medium-sized butterflies found in the eastern half of the United States, reaching areas as north as Nova Scotia, Canada. Not only are they the state butterfly of Maryland, but they have distinguishing patterns that set them apart from other orange and black butterflies. Orange crescents rest below rows of white dots adorning the edges of their black wings. Random spots of orange and white are also found closer to their bodies. Their antenna clubs are a matching orange, while the underside of their wings is similar in design to the top side. It's probably no surprise that Baltimore checkerspot caterpillars are also black and orange in appearance. Their plants of choice are white turtlehead and honeysuckle, while adult butterflies feed on the nectar of black-eyed Susan and common milkweed plants.

BY THE NUMBERS

A female Baltimore checkerspot may only have one brood a year, but she makes it count! She lays a cluster of 100-700 dome-shaped eggs at once under the common turtlehead host plant.

WINTER HANGOUTS

Checkerspot caterpillars hibernate together in groups by the base of their host plant by forming a web of debris and leaves stuck together with silk.

34. EASTERN TAILED-BLUE

Often mistaken for the blue morpho, eastern tailed-blues are small, delicate butterflies that seem to float through the air. Males have the characteristic royal blue color when their wings are open flat, while females display a brown hue. For both genders, the undersides of their wings are a pale blue with grayish markings. Slight orange markings are also displayed at the bottom of their hindwings. These vibrant creatures find their home in the eastern part of North America where there are weedy, sunny, and open areas with plenty of nectar. Eastern tailed-blues have a preference for white clover, shepherd's needle, winter cress, and wild strawberry. Caterpillars, on the other hand, are all about flowering and bean plants when it comes to meal time!

CLASSIFICATION

KINGDOM: *Animalia*

PHYLUM: *Arthropoda*

CLASS: *Insecta*

ORDER: *Lepidoptera*

FAMILY: *Lycaenidae*

GENUS: *Cupido*

SPECIES: *C. comyntas*

WINTER STAY

Three broods of eastern tailed-blues are born each year. The last group hibernates during winter. Where do you think they make their winter home? They overwinter in pea and bean pods!

LENGTH LINEUP

The eastern tailed-blue is much smaller than the world's largest butterfly, the Queen Alexandra's birdwing. With a wingspan of almost 12 inches, the Queen Alexandra is about 12 times the size of the eastern tailed-blue.

Domestic
Cattle

35. RED-SPOTTED PURPLE

The name of the red-spotted purple can be misleading. While a strikingly gorgeous butterfly, it is neither red, purple, nor spotted. Instead, the red-spotted purple actually has iridescent bluish-black hues with orange, white, and black spots on the wing borders. Mostly found from Texas to the eastern United States, red-spotted purples are large in size with a wingspan of up to 3.5 inches. Feeding on nectar is uncommon for red-spotted purples. Instead, adults prefer tree sap, dung, and rotting fruit. They inhabit forests and wooded suburban areas where there is both ample food and shelter. Active butterflies, the red-spotted purples fly at low altitudes of two to three feet or can otherwise be seen walking over leaves with their wings folded. Watch your step!

CLEVER DECEPTION

Red-spotted purples are known for their clever defense tactic called "Batesian mimicry." Their keen resemblance to the poisonous pipevine swallowtail butterfly helps them avoid being eaten by predators.

SOCIAL GATHERINGS

It is common for the red-spotted purple to gather with thousands of other butterfly species to drink from mud puddles and stream banks. While they tend to rest in high treetops, they will drop down for such festivities.

Woodland Grayling

MASTER OF DISGUISE

Graylings have adapted to their environment with cryptic coloration. The earth tones of their wings allow them to camouflage into their surroundings, reducing their likelihood of being attacked.

36. GRAYLING

Coastal habitats of England, Wales, Scotland, and Ireland are where you are most likely to find colonies of graylings. They like areas with sparse vegetation, well-drained soil, and dry heathlands. You can identify these medium-sized butterflies from their brown and tan forewings, pale orange splotches, and multiple eye spots. Their undersides are a combination of muted brown, gray, and white hues. Grayling butterflies are in flight from June to August, with occasional sightings into September where you can observe them in their looping and gliding flight. To help regulate their body temperature, graylings can be found sunbathing with their wings closed and the leading edge angled toward the sun.

CLASSIFICATION

KINGDOM: *Animalia*

PHYLUM: *Arthropoda*

CLASS: *Insecta*

ORDER: *Lepidoptera*

FAMILY: *Nymphalidae*

GENUS: *Hipparchia*

SPECIES: *H. semele*

CAMERA SHY

It can be difficult to catch a grayling feeding with enough time to snap a picture. As they don't feed often, you can increase your chances of a photo opportunity early in the morning or late afternoon.

A TASTE FOR GRASS

While the thought of a grass lunch might make you queasy, grayling caterpillars delight in a variety of grass meals like red fescue, sheep's fescue, and marram grass.

Rock Grayling

ALL IN THE FAMILY

There are multiple butterflies in the same family as the blue morpho. In fact, there are 29 "morpho" species ranging in colors from green, brown, and even a rare white species!

Achilles
Morpho

37. BLUE MORPHO

Vivid blue wings with black edging make the gorgeous blue morpho butterfly stand out against the bold colors of the Amazon rainforest canopies. One of the largest butterflies in the world, the blue morpho has a wingspan that can reach almost eight inches and is a clear favorite among butterfly enthusiasts. Interestingly, only the male butterflies are blue, which comes in handy during mating season. Highly territorial, male blue morphos use their brightly colored wings to intimidate other male competitors while remaining particularly visible to potential female mates. There are many cultures that find symbolic meaning in this unique species. Some believe that spotting a blue morpho means a wish will come true, while others believe that the butterfly is the host of a malevolent spirit.

CLASSIFICATION

KINGDOM: *Animalia*

PHYLUM: *Arthropoda*

CLASS: *Insecta*

ORDER: *Lepidoptera*

FAMILY: *Nymphalidae*

TRIBE: *Morphini*

GENUS: *Morpho*

FLASHING FLIGHT

Blue morphos utilize "flashing" as a method of self-defense. As they flap their wings, they alternate between the bright blue and dull brown of their undersides, making them hard to track by predators.

TRICKY TRICKSTERS

Similar to certain bird species, blue morphos exhibit a phenomenon called "iridescence." Light reflects off the microscopic scales on their wings, making them appear blue.

Adonis Morpho

PLAYING DEAD

One of the clever defense tactics of the common wood-nymph is to drop to the ground like a leaf if other efforts like eyespots are not warding off predators. Their camouflage colors can make such an action believable.

38. COMMON WOOD-NYMPH

Common wood-nymph butterflies are found in all the continental U.S. states and all the way north as Canada. Due to its name, you might expect wood-nymphs to only inhabit wooded areas. In actuality, they are highly adaptable and also flourish in tall grassy areas like fields, prairies, and wet meadows. These medium-sized butterflies are predominantly brown with various patterns. Common wood-nymphs have two eyespots on their forewings and a white pupil on each, with the lower eyespot often being larger than the upper eyespot. Hindwings can show no eyespots or many on either the dorsal or ventral sides. All varieties, however, tend to have a pale-yellow ring on the outside of each eyespot. Common wood-nymphs are not strong flyers and are more commonly spotted on flowers and near mud puddles.

CLEAR COMPARISON

How does the common wood-nymph compare in size to other butterfly species? They are smaller than the famous monarch or Canadian tiger swallowtail but larger than eastern tailed-blues.

ALTERNATE ALIAS

Similar to the common wood-nymph, you might also have a nickname. Some of their nicknames are goggle eye, large wood nymph, and blue-eyed grayling.

Large Blue

UNIQUE DIFFERENCES

Male Alcon blues are a deep blue color with a black border and black spots. Females, on the other hand, are light brown, with black spots and a blue basal area.

1

2

Alcon Blue

2

Large
Blue

74

39. ALCON BLUE

Like many butterflies in the *Lycaenidae* family, Alcon blues are large blue butterflies that have a relationship with ants. It's a defining trait along with their unusual life cycle. After the short egg stage on flowers of the marsh gentian plant, the larvae will sometimes continue their development in the nests of *Myrmica* ants. The caterpillar secretes a sweet substance that ants enjoy, causing them to adopt and carry the caterpillar back to their nest. From here, the caterpillars become a parasite, with ants feeding them instead of their own young, making for smaller ant colonies. After about 23 months underground, the Alcon blue will have gained 100 times its original weight in preparation to pupate. Once it emerges as an adult, the Alcon blue leaves the nest.

CLASSIFICATION

KINGDOM: *Animalia*

PHYLUM: *Arthropoda*

CLASS: *Insecta*

ORDER: *Lepidoptera*

FAMILY: *Lycaenidae*

GENUS: *Phengaris*

SPECIES: *P. alcon*

WIDE DISTRIBUTION

While you won't find an Alcon blue in the United States, there are plenty of other places to discover them. Alcon blues inhabit areas of Europe and the northern parts of the Eastern Hemisphere.

MEETING AREA

Alcon blues, after sufficiently feeding on their host plant, will leave and head for the ground. Here, they will wait to be discovered by ants while emitting chemicals that mimic ant larvae to draw them closer.

ABOUT THE AUTHOR

Christin is the author of several books for kids, including many in the Little Library of Natural History. She lives with her family in California, where she enjoys rollerblading, puzzles, and a good book.